FULL STEAM BASKETBALL

Science, Technology, Engineering, Arts, and Mathematics of the Game

by N. Helget

CAPSTONE PRESS
a capstone imprint

Fact Finders Books are published by Capstone Press
1710 Roe Crest Drive, North Mankato, Minnesota 56003
www.mycapstone.com

Library of Congress Cataloging-in-Publication Data
Names: Helget, Nicole Lea, 1976– author.
Title: Full STEAM basketball : science, technology, engineering, arts, and mathematics of the game / by N. Helget.
Description: North Mankato, Minnesota : Capstone Press, 2019. | Series: Fact finders. Full STEAM sports | Audience: Age 8–14.
Identifiers: LCCN 2018016136 (print) | LCCN 2018019630 (ebook) | ISBN 9781543530452 (eBook PDF) | ISBN 9781543530377 (hardcover) | ISBN 9781543530414 (pbk.)
Subjects: LCSH: Basketball—Juvenile literature. | Sports sciences—Juvenile literature. | Sports—Technological innovations—Juvenile literature. Classification: LCC GV885.1 (ebook) | LCC GV885.1 .H444 2019 (print) | DDC 796.323—dc23
LC record available at https://lccn.loc.gov/2018016136

Editorial Credits
Editor: Nate LeBoutillier
Designer: Terri Poburka
Media Researcher: Eric Gohl
Production Specialist: Kris Wilfahrt

Photo Credits
Alamy: PCN Photography, 17; AP Photo: Al Behrman, 14, Jason DeCrow, 29, Michael Okoniewski, 12; Dreamstime: Scott Anderson, 10, Shariff Che\' Lah, 22; Getty Images: Bettmann, 18; Library of Congress: 19, 23; Newscom: Cal Sport Media/Thurman James, 27, EFE/Craig Lassig, cover, Icon Sportswire/Brian Rothmuller, 6, MCT/Carlos Gonzalez, 25 (bottom), Splash News/Matt Thorpe, 9, TNS/Minneapolis Star Tribune, 24, UPI/Bill Greenblatt, 20, USA Today Sports/Isaiah J. Downing, 15, USA Today Sports/David Butler II, 21, USA Today Sports/Jesse Johnson, 25 (top), USA Today Sports/Mark D. Smith, 4, USA Today Sports/Troy Taormina, 13; Shutterstock: Alex_Alekseev, 28, Benguhan, 7 (player), dovla982, 7 (hoop), Jamie Lamor Thompson, 11, Nicku, 8

Design Elements
Shutterstock

Printed in the United States 4747

CONTENTS

INTRODUCTION

AN INVENTIVE GAME

Russell Westbrook is a guard for the Oklahoma City Thunder.

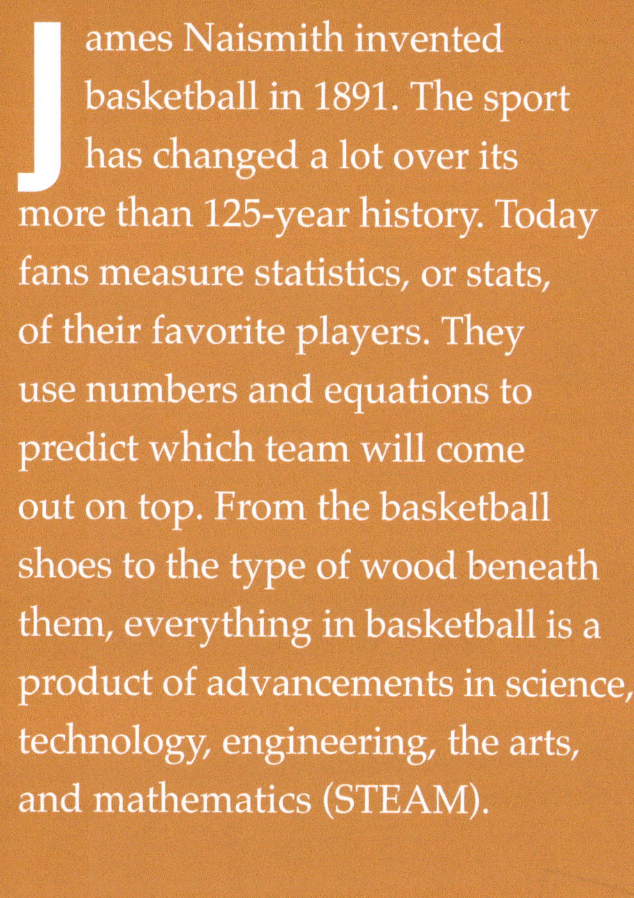

James Naismith invented basketball in 1891. The sport has changed a lot over its more than 125-year history. Today fans measure statistics, or stats, of their favorite players. They use numbers and equations to predict which team will come out on top. From the basketball shoes to the type of wood beneath them, everything in basketball is a product of advancements in science, technology, engineering, the arts, and mathematics (STEAM).

CHAPTER ONE

SCIENCE

PHYSICS: The Perfect Three-Pointer

Physics professor Gintaras Duda studies basketball players and makes calculations. He says the perfect shot comes down to **angle**, **velocity**, and the **Magnus effect**.

Speed and angle are important in sinking a three-pointer.

Duda learned the lowest possible angle, or arc, for a three-point shot is 33 degrees. The angle with the best chance of sinking that ball through the rim is 45 degrees. The speed the ball travels comes from the force of the shot by the player. The ball must travel a little under 20 miles per hour for a three-pointer. Lastly, a backspin of two revolutions per second gives the ball enough lift. This effect is explained by the Magnus effect. Spinning changes the airflow around the ball to create an arc rather than a flat line.

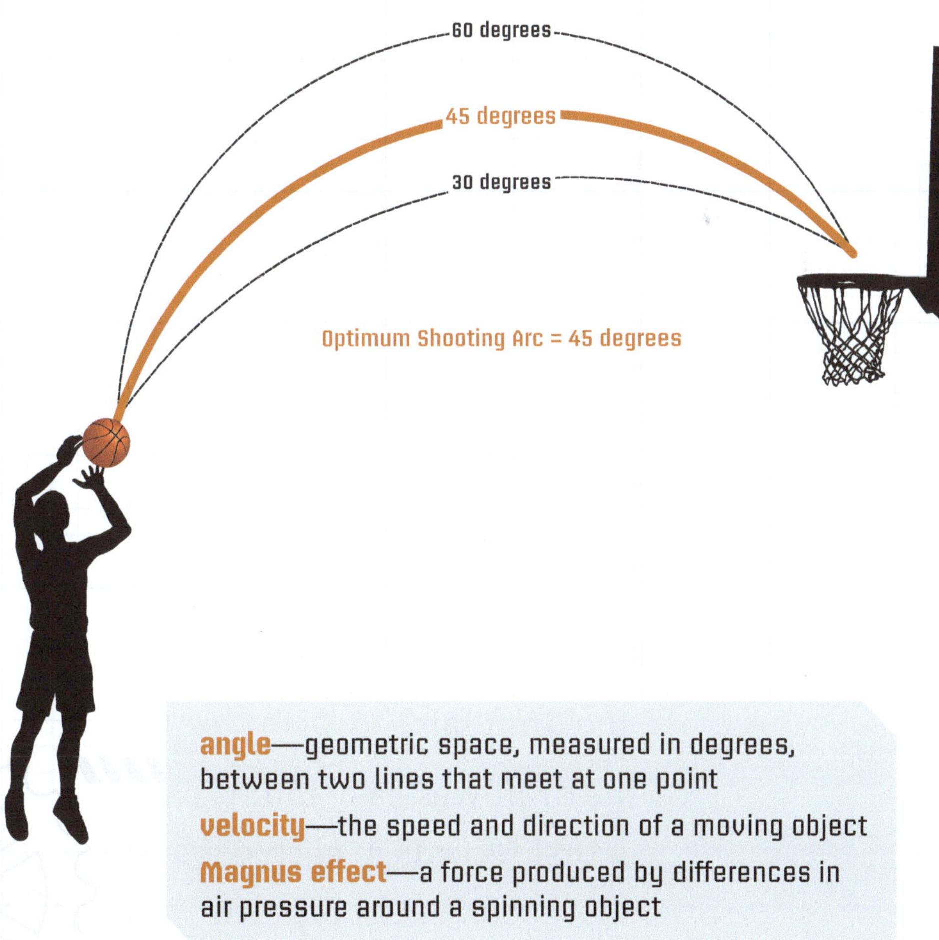

angle—geometric space, measured in degrees, between two lines that meet at one point

velocity—the speed and direction of a moving object

Magnus effect—a force produced by differences in air pressure around a spinning object

NEWTON'S LAW OF MOTION: What Makes a Basketball Bounce?

Newton's Third Law of Motion is at work in dribbling a basketball. A **force** is a push or a pull on an object. Forces always come in pairs. Consider this example: Boston Celtics star Kyrie Irving crouches and pushes the ball to the floor hard in a low dribble. This is a downward force. Smack! The floor returns the ball to his fingertips in a bounce.

Sir Isaac Newton

By exerting an upward force on the ball, the floor is "passing" the ball to Irving. Newton's third law says "For every action, there is an equal and opposite reaction." The ball going down from the hand, object one, is force one. There must be an equal and opposite reaction. So when the ball hits object two, the floor, it is sent up and back to the hand by force two.

Not many can dribble like Kyrie Irving, left, of the Boston Celtics. He is widely considered the best dribbler in the NBA today.

If the ball were **dense**, like a bowling ball, it wouldn't return to the hand. But the floor would still react. With the impact of a heavy ball, the floor indents, and waves of vibration circle out from the point of impact.

force—factors (like pushing or pulling) that cause something to change its speed

dense—containing a lot of matter in a small space

HEALTH: Compression Clothing

On January 21, 2001, Allen Iverson injured his elbow. His trainer slipped a very tight sleeve over his aching arm. Iverson hopped off the bench, entered the game, and scored 51 points that night.

Did this **compression** sleeve help Iverson? Or was his shooting success that night a fluke? Either way, after Iverson first wore one in 2001, ballers on every court started using compression clothing—shorts, undershirts, socks, tights, and sleeves.

Allen Iverson

Kinesiology is the study of movement. In sports this field focuses on athlete performance. Some researchers are studying if and how compression clothing helps athletes. Compression garments are very tight. They are usually made of elastin and nylon.

Maya Moore

Researchers think the squeezing of muscles and joints may apply enough pressure to decrease swelling and prevent pain. Researchers also study whether compression garments increase blood flow. Many athletes think this special clothing improves their speed and helps injuries heal.

compression—a squishing force

CHAPTER TWO

TECHNOLOGY

COMPUTERS AND SOFTWARE: The Shot Clock

In 1950 fans watched the Minneapolis Lakers and the Fort Wayne Pistons. Fans yawned. They booed. Before the game ended, many fans left.

Why? Because the Pistons held the ball. They passed it around. They didn't shoot. The Pistons didn't want to do anything to allow the best team in the league a chance at the ball. At the final buzzer, the Pistons won 19–18.

Former NBA owner Danny Biasone invented the 24-second shot clock.

In 1954 the shot clock entered the pro game. At the start of each new ball possession, the offensive team had 24 seconds to shoot. If the team failed to take a shot, the ball went to the other team.

James Harden of the Houston Rockets beats the shot clock.

The shot clock stopped players from stalling or ball-hogging. Games included more shots, faster action, and better strategy. In just one season's time, teams that had usually scored less than 80 points per game began to average more than 90 points per game.

TRAINING ADVANCEMENTS: Strobe Glasses

Stephen Curry dribbles a basketball with his right hand. At the same time, with his left hand, he tosses a tennis ball to his trainer. The trainer tosses it back, and Curry catches it. Curry wears vision-altering goggles. These glasses blink one lens at a time or flash alternately or blind him completely. Curry's **agility** is due to training his brainpower.

Strobe glasses are used to help hand-eye coordination in various training exercises.

Stephen Curry (right) uses high-tech training to improve his skills on the court.

Curry was first known for his shooting skills. Now he is also one of the NBA's best ball handlers. Curry can thank technological advancements and practice. Curry's trainer calls the workouts "**neuromuscular** efficiency." That means Curry is training his eyes to take in and process information as quickly as possible. That way his brain quickly sends signals to his legs, arms, hands, and fingers.

agility—the ability to move in a quick and easy way
neuromuscular—relating to both nerves and muscles

THE EVOLUTION OF THE BASKETBALL SNEAKER: Safer and Springier

A typical NBA basketball player puts 700 pounds of pressure on his foot with every stride. While jumping, the pounds of pressure can exceed 1,200. In 1977 an **aeronautical engineer** named M. Frank Rudy had an idea. He approached Nike with a design for a new kind of sole.

Rudy explained that all materials degrade and break down. So shoe soles have less cushion over time. But, he said, **molecules** of air don't degrade. They don't break down. And, they're light, which is very important for a leaping shooter.

In this way, Nike Air, a shoe with captured air in the heel, was born. Soon, a famous player named Michael Jordan sported the sneakers. The shoes became known as Air Jordans.

aeronautical—relating to the science of flight

engineer—a person who has scientific training and who designs

molecule—group of two or more atoms bonded together

Michael Jordan is known as one of the best NBA players of all time.

CHAPTER THREE

ENGINEERING

MATERIALS: How Soccer Balls, Peach Baskets, and Farm Equipment Made the Game

In 1891 James Naismith's game used peach baskets and a soccer ball. He soon realized the equipment needed an upgrade. He asked engineers to design a ball. The new ball would be bigger. The texture of the ball changed from smooth to bumpy. The tiny bumps increase the **friction** between players' hands and the surface of the ball.

Dr. James Naismith, inventor of the game of basketball

A basketball rim today still looks a little like a peach basket. The original baskets were made of thin wood and woven together in a net pattern. In 1925 the first pro basketball league had hoops with backboards, metal rims, and nets that were open at the end.

Changing the texture of the basketball made it easier for players to grip.

In the 1970s, it was time to update the basketball rim. Players who dunked the ball often shattered backboards and broke rims. A man from Illinois named Arthur Ehrat took a spring off an old farm machine and put it on a backboard and a pole. A spring is a coil of metal. It stretches when pulled but returns to its original shape when it's let go. Ehrat's engineering was the first breakaway rim. In 1982 the NBA said all pro courts must use these types of rims.

friction—a force created when two objects rub together; friction slows down objects

CIVIL ENGINEERING: Why Are Courts Made of Wood?

The wooden boards of a basketball court look like a puzzle. The boards are made of wood from maple trees. The wood is dense, which means it doesn't splinter much. The **grains** of the board are tight, which makes them hard enough to return energy for dribbling and running. If the wood absorbs too much energy, dribbles don't pop back. Running players tire faster because the floor soaks up their footfalls like mud.

Workers lift one of the 200 or more panels of a court surface in preparation for a game.

The Boston Celtics' court is one of the most recognizable in the NBA.

On the other hand, the wood has to be soft enough to absorb some shock from hard bounce passes or a jumping player with as little vibration as possible.

The original Boston Garden, where the Celtics used to play, was known for its court. Players from visiting teams disliked its "dead spots." The ball didn't bounce well in these places. The wood in the dead spots absorbed the force of the ball more than in other places on the court. The dead spots led to turnovers. Teams said the court gave the Celtics an advantage. In the 1985–86 season, the Celtics won 40 of their 41 games at home in the Garden.

grain—the way the lines or fibers in something (such as wood) are arranged

CHAPTER FOUR

ARTS

THEATER: Basketball as Performance Art

The Harlem Globetrotters are both a basketball team and a traveling **theater**. Begun in 1928 by Abe Saperstein, the Globetrotters' popularity spread across America. Excellent athletes, the players are tricksters and entertainers on the court.

Flight Time Lang entertains a young fan at a game in 2009.

No-look passes, between-the-legs dribbling, alley-oops, and leaping dunks were developed by men like Reece "Goose" Tatum and Wilt "The Stilt" Chamberlain. The Globetrotters influence today's top players.

The great Wilt Chamberlain played with the Harlem Globetrotters in 1958–59.

Before the Globetrotters, court showmanship was frowned upon. It wasn't polite to dribble a basketball through one's legs, much less through the legs of an opposing player. But next time you see a behind-the-back pass, you can thank the theater of the Globetrotters.

theater—the art or activity of performing, as in a play

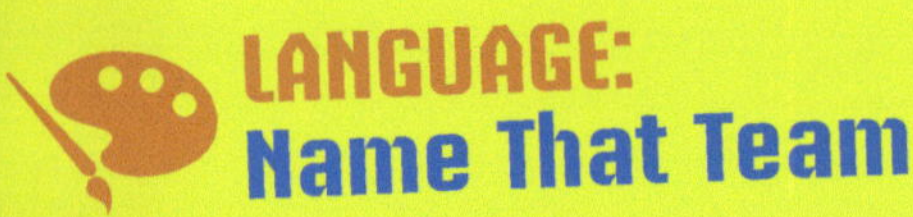

LANGUAGE: Name That Team

The New Orleans Jazz. The Atlanta Hawks. The Chicago Bulls. The Orlando Magic. The Miami Heat. Where do teams get their names? A team name often has a story to tell.

From the pine forests to the blue lakes, Minnesotans love nature. It makes sense that their first basketball team was called the Lakers. In 1947 team owners chose the name because the state's motto is "Land of 10,000 Lakes."

Bud Grant played for the Minneapolis Lakers.

Karl-Anthony Towns of the Minnesota Timberwolves

In 1960 the team moved to Los Angeles. In 1989 a new team came to Minnesota. Cities throughout the state got to vote on the name. The name "Timberwolves" was chosen. Minnesota has the largest population of timber wolves in the lower 48 states.

In 1999 a pro women's basketball team came to Minnesota. Named the Lynx, it is a nod to the Timberwolves. Timber wolves are in the canine family. Lynx are wildcats. Both animals are tough and fierce. Both do well in winter, which is the season when basketball is played.

Lindsay Whalen plays for the Minnesota Lynx.

CHAPTER FIVE

MATHEMATICS

π COMPUTER LEARNING: The Pick and Roll

Rajiv Maheswaran studies a screen. Each dot is a basketball player on the court. The dots replay the pick and roll play.

Maheswaran leads a company that uses video tracking to help teams improve. He collects and analyzes the data behind the pick and roll.

The pick and roll involves two offensive players and one or two defensive players. One of the offensive players, the screener, stops in front of a defender to prevent him from following the ball handler. This is the "pick." The offensive ball handler skirts around the defender. Then the screener rolls around the defender to accept a pass from the ball handler. The screener takes the pass and scores a basket.

Players can do this move in many ways. Coaches wanted to know which way was best. But the pick and roll happens fast. It's hard for a coach to study the move during a game.

The pick and roll is a difficult play for defenses to try and contain, as shown here by Mikayla Cowling (3) and Penina Davidson (12) of the University of California in 2018.

Maheswaran's computers can show details missed by a coach. Video technology slows down the play. It shows a closer view of players' movements. And it interprets the data using equations like percentages. This way coaches can see which players are best at the play. They can decide the best times to run a pick and roll.

PROBABILITY: What Are the Odds?

In the NBA **draft**, teams select college's best players. Every team wants them. How can the NBA make the draft fair?

Before 1985 the draft was easy math. The two NBA teams with the worst records in each conference were given a shot at first pick. A coin flip decided. The **probability** formula for a coin flip looks like this: ½ = .50 (50 percent). The team that won the coin flip got the first draft pick. The team that lost got the second. There was a problem, though. Teams with poor records wanted to keep losing at the end of a season. After all, there was a reward for being last.

In 1985 the NBA changed the draft to a lottery system. The 14 teams not in the playoffs are given a certain amount of combinations with the numbers 1 to 14.

draft—an event in which athletes are picked to join sports organizations or teams

probability—how likely or unlikely it is for something to happen

Each NBA draft pick gives unsuccessful NBA teams hope that they will land the best new players in the game.

The team with the worst record gets the most combinations, 250 of 1,000. This makes that team's odds of getting the winning combination 25 percent. The team with the best record is given only five combinations. That team's odds of getting the winning combination is just 0.5 percent.

Fourteen balls, numbered 1 to 14, tumble inside a barrel. One at a time, four balls are pulled. The team with those numbers gets the first draft pick. The process is repeated two more times for the second and third picks. After that teams get to make a draft pick in inverse order of their record.

GLOSSARY

aeronautical (air-oh-NAHT-uh-kohl)—relating to the science of flight

agility (uh-GI-luh-tee)—the ability to move in a quick and easy way

angle (ANG-uhl)—geometric space, measured in degrees, between two lines that meet at one point

compression (kuhm-PRE-shuhn)—a squishing force

dense (DENS)—containing a lot of matter in a small space

draft (DRAFT)—an event in which athletes are picked to join sports organizations or teams

engineer (en-juh-NEER)—a person who has scientific training and who designs

force (FORS)—factors (like pushing or pulling) that cause something to change its speed

friction (FRIK-shuhn)—a force created when two objects rub together; friction slows down objects

grain (GRAYN)—the way the lines or fibers in something (such as wood) are arranged

Magnus effect (MAG-nuhs uf-FEKT)—a force produced by differences in air pressure around a spinning object

molecule (MOL-uh-kyool)—group of two or more atoms bonded together

neuromuscular (NOO-roh-MUHSS-cue-lar)—relating to both nerves and muscles

probability (PROB-uh-bulh-uh-tee)—how likely or unlikely it is for something to happen

theater (THEE-uh-tur)—the art or activity of performing, as in a play

velocity (vuh-LOSS-uh-tee)—the speed and direction of a moving object

READ MORE

Buckley, James, Jr. *STEM in Sports. Technology*. STEM in Sports. Broomall, Penn.: Mason Crest, 2015.

Graubart, Norman D. *The Science of Basketball*. Sports Science. New York: PowerKids Press, 2016.

INTERNET SITES

Use FactHound to find Internet sites related to this book.

Visit www.facthound.com.

Just type in 9781543530377 and go.

Check out projects, games and lots more at **www.capstonekids.com**

INDEX